— CONTINENTS —
AFRICA

Linda Aspen-Baxter

W

WEIGL PUBLISHERS INC.

Published by Weigl Publishers Inc.
350 5th Avenue, Suite 3304, PMB 6G
New York, NY 10118-0069 USA
Web site: www.weigl.com

Library of Congress Cataloging-in-Publication Data

Aspen-Baxter, Linda.
  Africa / Linda Aspen-Baxter.
    p. cm. -- (Continents)
  Includes index.
  ISBN 1-59036-316-7 (hard cover : alk. paper) -- ISBN 1-59036-323-X (soft
cover : alk. paper)
  1. Africa--Juvenile literature. I. Title. II. Continents (New York, N.Y.)
  DT3.A85 2005
  960--dc22

                                        2005003965

Printed in the United States of America
1 2 3 4 5 6 7 8 9 10 09 08 07 06 05

Photograph Credits
Every reasonable effort has been made to trace ownership and to obtain
permission to reprint copyright material. The publishers would be pleased
to have any errors or omissions brought to their attention so that they may
be corrected in subsequent printings.

Cover: Africa's Sahara Desert is the largest hot desert in the world. (David
Jones/Stone/Getty Images)

Getty Images: pages 1 (The Image Bank), 4-5 (Panoramic Images), 6L
(Ira Rubin/Taxi), 6TR (Frans Lemmens/The Image Bank), 6BR (Gallo
Images), 8 (The Image Bank), 9 (Stone), 10 (Taxi), 11R (FoodPix), 11L
(Richard Dobson/Taxi), 12 (Richard Dobson/Taxi/Getty Images), Inset (Kenneth
Garrett/National Geographic/Getty Images), 13 (Photodisc Red), 14 (Dag
Sundberg/The Image Bank), 15B (Michael Lewis/National Geographic), 15T
(The Image Bank), 16 (Photographer's Choice), 17 (Hulton Archive), 18 (Hulton
Archive), 19T (Time Life Pictures/Mansell/Time Life Pictures), 19B (Hulton
Archive), 20 (Ami Vitale), 21 (Frank Micelotta), 22 (Stone), 23L (Art Wolfe/The
Image Bank), 23R (Eric Meola/TheImage Bank), 24 (Harvey Lloyd/Taxi), 25R
(The Image Bank), 25L (Ellen Rooney/Robert Harding World Imagery), 26
(Khaled Dessouki/AFP), 27 (Clive Brunskill), 28L (Photographer's Choice),
28R (Anwar Hussein), 29L (Photographer's Choice), 29R (Stone), 30 (The
Image Bank), 31 (Brand X Pictures).

Project Coordinator
Heather C. Hudak

Copy Editor
Tina Schwartzenberger

Designer
Terry Paulhus

Layout
Gregg Muller
Kathryn Livingstone

Photo Researcher
Kim Winiski

— CONTINENTS —

AFRICA

TABLE OF CONTENTS

Introduction 4

Africa........................... 6

Location and Resources

    Land and Climate 8

    Plants and Animals 10

    Natural Resources 11

Economy

    Tourism.......................... 12

    Industry 14

    Goods and Services 15

The Past

    Indigenous Peoples 16

    The Age of Exploration............... 17

    Early Settlers 18

Culture

    Population 20

    Politics and Government 21

    Cultural Groups 22

    Arts and Entertainment.............. 24

    Sports 26

Brain Teasers...................... 28

For More Information 30

Glossary 31

Index 32

Introduction

*A*frica is a continent of amazing contrasts. Vast areas of sand and gravel, lush tropical rain forests, and sweeping grasslands cover the continent. Africa is home to many plants and animals that people from other parts of the world see only in zoos.

With many unique cultures, Africa's peoples and their ways of life are as varied as the land. Some groups still live as their ancestors lived hundreds of years ago. Many other cultures live a less traditional way of life by learning how to use new technologies.

Africa's land is very rich in resources, but many people die of starvation and disease. This land of beauty and wonder is also a land of much poverty and need.

With fifty-three independent countries and other **political units**, Africa has more countries than any other continent. Sudan is the biggest country in Africa, with 967,490 square miles (2,505,800 square kilometers) of land. At 175 square miles (454 sq km), Seychelles is the smallest country. With a total of about 137,000,000 people, the country with the highest population is Nigeria, followed by Egypt and Ethiopia.

Many Africans are well known for helping others. Nelson Mandela received the 1993 Nobel Peace Prize for his work to end racism and **apartheid** in South Africa. In 1994, Mandela became the first democratically elected president of South Africa. Kenyan runner Kipchoge "Kip" Keino amazed onlookers by winning the 1,500-meter gold medal and 5,000-meter silver medal at the 1968 Summer Olympics. *Sports Illustrated* named Kip one of the "Sportsmen of the Year" in 1987 for his work with orphaned and abandoned children. Somalian Waris Dirie is an international supermodel, actress, and human rights **ambassador** for the United Nations. She helps protect the rights of female children in African countries.

Traditional north African foods include **falafel**, flat bread with **hummus**, and **couscous**. South of the Sahara Desert, **plantains** are fried or cooked with porridge. A traditional African meal often includes rice or yams served with a vegetable and meat sauce.

The Masai Mara National Reserve is located in the Great Rift Valley. It stretches from Ethiopia's Red Sea through Kenya, Tanzania, Malawi, and Mozambique. Giraffes are just some of the animals that roam the park.

Africa

Africa stretches nearly 5,000 miles (8,100 km) from north to south and about 4,700 miles (7,600 km) from east to west. It is the world's second largest continent. The **equator** divides Africa. Part of the continent sits in the Northern **Hemisphere**, and part sits in the Southern Hemisphere.

Water surrounds Africa on all sides. The 80-mile (130-km) wide Sinai Peninsula in Egypt connects Africa to Asia. If not for this narrow land connection, Africa would be an island.

On its northern coast, the Mediterranean Ocean separates Africa from Europe. The Atlantic Ocean borders Africa along its west and south coasts. The Indian Ocean borders the continent on its south and east coasts.

Fast Facts

Algeria is the second-largest country in Africa in terms of land. Only Sudan is larger.

There are 800,000 miles (1,300,000 km) of roads in Africa, but less than one-tenth are paved. Most people travel by bus, foot, or ride bicycles.

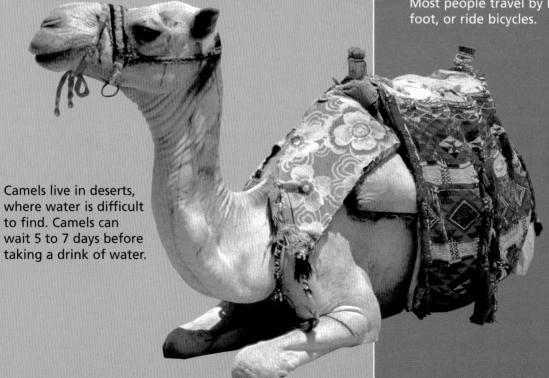

Camels live in deserts, where water is difficult to find. Camels can wait 5 to 7 days before taking a drink of water.

African Continent Map

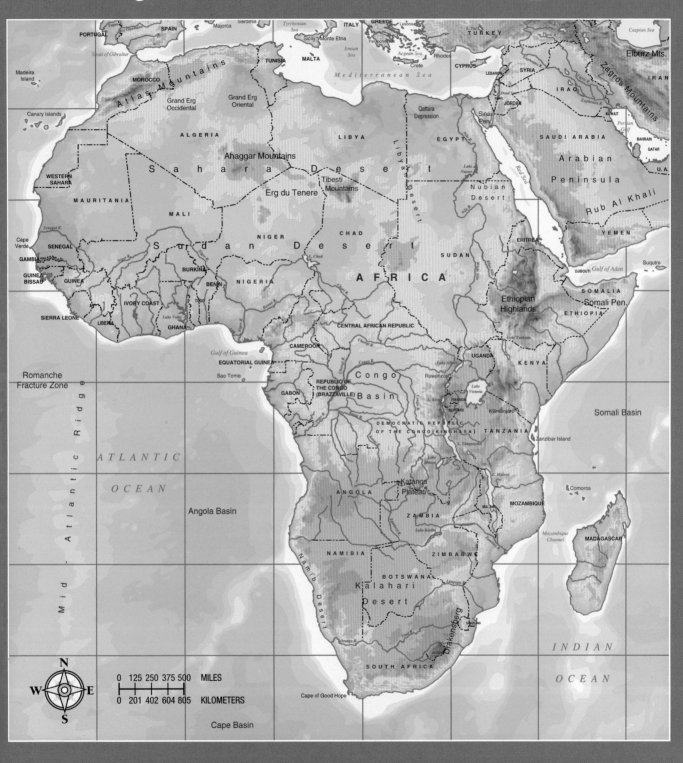

Location and Resources

Land and Climate

Africa covers about 11,700,000 square miles (30,200,000 sq km), or one-fifth, of Earth. Africa is an enormous **plateau** with a few mountain ranges. Deserts, tropical rain forests, and grasslands cover most of the continent.

Very dry deserts cover about two-fifths of Africa. Some desert areas receive less than 10 inches (25 centimeters) of rain each year. In other desert regions, rain may not fall for 6 or 7 years. The Sahara Desert stretches across northern Africa from the Atlantic Ocean to the Red Sea. It is the world's largest desert. In this desert, bare rock, gravel plains, and sand dunes cover an area of 3.5 million square miles (9 million sq km). The Namib and Kalahari Deserts are found in southwest Africa.

The Samburu are an ancient culture. They continue to practice their traditional way of life south of Lake Turkana in the Rift Valley Province of Kenya.

Grasslands called savannahs cover more than two-fifths of Africa. Thorny bushes, tall grasses, and scattered trees dot the land. Savannahs stretch from the western coast just south of the Sahara Desert across eastern Africa and back to the Atlantic coast south of the Congo Basin.

Many of Africa's forests are tropical rain forests. Tropical rain forests receive as much as 400 inches (1000 cm) of rainfall each year—more than any other place on Earth. Rain forests once grew across much of central Africa. Today, they are found mainly in the Congo Basin, parts of western Africa, and Madagascar. It rains throughout the year in the rain forests of the Congo Basin and coastal regions of western Africa.

The most mountainous region in Africa is the Great Rift Valley. It extends from Mozambique to Israel along the eastern coast. This long valley with many lakes and volcanoes formed centuries ago.

Africa has the largest tropical area of any continent. Most of the continent lies between the Tropic of Capricorn and the Tropic of Cancer. These areas border the equator. Temperatures are high—often reaching higher than 80° Fahrenheit (30° Celsius) throughout the year in many parts of the continent. The coolest regions of Africa are in the northwest, the highland areas of the east, and parts of the south. Temperatures in these places are between 60° and 70° F (16° and 21° C).

Fast Facts

The seasons in countries south of the equator are opposite to those in countries north of the equator. June and July are Africa's coolest months.

The Nile River is the world's longest river. It is 4,160 miles (6,695 km) long.

Africa's largest lake is Lake Victoria. It covers 26,828 square miles (69,484 sq km) of land.

Elephants live in the Amboseli National Park near Mount Kilimanjaro in Tanzania.

Plants and Animals

Africa's tropical rain forests are home to hundreds of trees species, such as oil palms, fruit trees, ebony, mahogany, and **okoumé**. Mangrove trees are found along the tropical coasts.

Tall grasses, baobab trees, acacia trees, and thorny bushes grow on savannahs. Some plants, such as date palms, doug palms, and acacias, can be found in an **oasis** or a dry riverbed.

In Africa's mountainous highlands, bamboo thickets, tree ferns, and cedar trees grow on the lower slopes. Grassy meadows grow higher on the slopes. Mosses and lichens grow near the top.

Africa's tropical rain forests are the only place on Earth where okapis live in nature. Okapis are related to giraffes, but smaller. They have a short neck, reddish-brown body, and white stripes on their legs. Monkeys, tree frogs, snakes, parrots, hornbills, and butterflies make their homes in the rain forests. Crocodiles and hippopotamuses live in tropical rivers and swamps.

Herds of gazelles, giraffes, zebras, cheetahs, hyenas, and lions roam the savannahs. Horned vipers, sand foxes, springboks, ostriches, and vultures live in the desert.

The okapi is the only mammal that is able to clean its own ears with its tongue.

Natural Resources

Agricultural products are very important to Africa's people. About two-thirds of Africans live in rural areas. They earn money by growing crops, such as cassava, yams, sorghum, millet, maize, and rice. They also earn money by raising livestock, such as goats, cattle, and sheep. Africa produces most of the world's cassava, cocoa beans, and yams. Cotton is also a major **export** crop grown across Africa.

Water is available in large quantities in some parts of Africa. Some areas suffer from severe **drought**, which makes farming very difficult. Since the 1960s, millions of Africans have died from starvation caused by drought in Ethiopia and the southern edge of the Sahara Desert. In areas with too much rainfall, the heavy rains wash away nourishing substances in the soil. Insects thrive in the hot, **humid** air. Some of these insects kill livestock and cause diseases in people.

Africa has many minerals, including copper, diamonds, gold, and petroleum. Half of the world's gold comes from Africa. Africa also has large amounts of diamonds, uranium, bauxite, phosphates, iron ore, chromite, manganese, cobalt, titanium, and platinum. Some parts of Africa are rich in mineral resources, while others have limited resources.

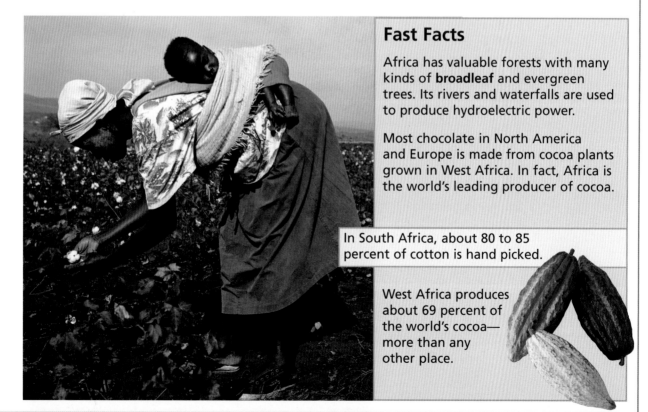

Fast Facts

Africa has valuable forests with many kinds of **broadleaf** and evergreen trees. Its rivers and waterfalls are used to produce hydroelectric power.

Most chocolate in North America and Europe is made from cocoa plants grown in West Africa. In fact, Africa is the world's leading producer of cocoa.

In South Africa, about 80 to 85 percent of cotton is hand picked.

West Africa produces about 69 percent of the world's cocoa— more than any other place.

Economy

Tourism

Many African countries, including South Africa, Kenya, Botswana, Tanzania, Zambia, and Rwanda, have huge national parks, game reserves, and animal parks. Many visitors take **safaris** at these parks and reserves each year. Safaris are hunting expeditions or guided tours of animals in their natural surroundings. Some parks and reserves feature savannah animals. Others provide an opportunity for people to see Africa's rain forest or desert animals.

The Cradle of Humankind is a World Heritage Site in South Africa. At this site, and others in eastern and southern Africa, visitors can see bones and other fossils that suggest the first humans lived in this part of Africa before moving to other parts of the world. At the Valley of Ancient Voices on the Eastern Cape, rock art and **artifacts** show how animals and people once used the valley as a shelter and a place of spiritual importance.

Dr. Robert Broom discovered the first adult ape-man fossils in 1936 in the Sterkfontein Caves. Some of the fossils in this cave are believed to be 3.5 million years old.

Ancient Egypt was the first African civilization and is an important part of world history. Egypt is home to the pyramids and temples that stand as a reminder of this important civilization. Built between 2700 and 2500 BC, many of the pyramids of Egypt are located in Giza, on the west bank of the Nile River near Cairo. The largest pyramid, or the Great Pyramid, was built for the Pharaoh Khufu. Tourists to Egypt can take a desert trek or sail on a cruise down the Nile River.

Visitors can enjoy traditional African life on an overnight stay at the Lesedi Cultural Village near Johannesburg, South Africa. This traditional village includes the traditions of the Basotho, Ndebele, Pedi, Xhosa, and Zulu peoples.

Cape Town, South Africa, offers a taste of life near the ocean. Tourists can visit the waterfront and see life in a working harbor. The Two Oceans Aquarium features the fish, **invertebrates**, mammals, reptiles, birds, and plants that live in the waters off the South African coastline.

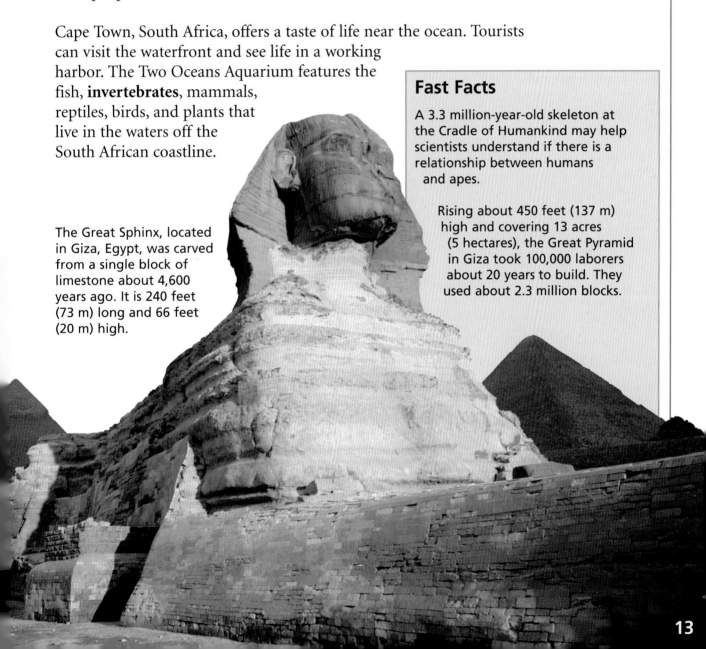

The Great Sphinx, located in Giza, Egypt, was carved from a single block of limestone about 4,600 years ago. It is 240 feet (73 m) long and 66 feet (20 m) high.

Fast Facts

A 3.3 million-year-old skeleton at the Cradle of Humankind may help scientists understand if there is a relationship between humans and apes.

Rising about 450 feet (137 m) high and covering 13 acres (5 hectares), the Great Pyramid in Giza took 100,000 laborers about 20 years to build. They used about 2.3 million blocks.

Industry

About half of northern Africans live in rural areas. They raise livestock or grow crops, such as wheat and barley. In the grasslands of eastern and southern Africa, farmers grow peanuts, corn, millet, and sorghum. In the wet, tropical areas of western and central Africa, farmers grow bananas, plantains, rice, yams, and cassava. Farmers also sell crops, such as coffee, cacao or cocoa beans, cotton, coconuts, and fruit.

More than half of the total value of Africa's exports comes from mining. Still, mines employ less than 1.5 million workers. South Africa, Libya, Nigeria, Algeria, and Zambia produce about 80 percent of all the minerals Africa exports.

Africa has about 25 percent of the world's forests, but only 15 percent of these forests are used for timber and wood products. Most of the cut wood is used for cooking fuel. The forest industry is very important in Cameroon, Congo (Brazzaville), Congo (Kinshasa), Côte d'Ivoire, Gabon, Ghana, and Nigeria. The most valuable trees are African walnut, mahogany, eucalyptus, and okoumé.

Along the coasts of Africa, fishers catch anchovies, mackerel, sardines, tuna, and other fish. Most of their catch is made into fish oil and fish meal for export to other countries.

Coffee was first found in eastern Africa in the area now known as Ethiopia.

Fast Facts

Africa raises more than two-thirds of the world's camels, nearly one-third of its goats, and about one-seventh of its cattle and sheep.

Africa produces about three-quarters of the world's cobalt and platinum.

Little manufacturing occurs in Africa. Large cities and towns are developing small industries that make products such as beer, cigarettes, furniture, shoes, soap, and soft drinks. Some factories make automobile parts and textiles.

South Africa produces about two-fifths of Africa's manufactured goods.

Goods and Services

Many African countries depend on one or two farm or mineral products for most of the money they earn from exports. For example, Libya and Nigeria rely mainly on petroleum. Botswana depends on diamonds, and Gambia has a strong peanut crop. Ghana grows cocoa, and Uganda harvests coffee crops. These countries suffer when crops fail or prices drop on the world market.

Africa trades mainly with Europe, Japan, and the United States. Little trade occurs between African countries. Africa's major imports include food, manufactured goods, transportation equipment, iron and steel, machinery, and motor vehicles. Their main exports are petroleum, cocoa, gold, coffee, and natural gas. South Africa is the most important petroleum-refining center in Africa. Peanuts are a major African crop, especially in the western tropical regions.

The United Nations provides millions of dollars in aid to many African countries. France, Great Britain, and the United States give more to Africa than many other nations. This aid helps build industries and houses, and improve agriculture.

Teff is a tiny grain native to northern Africa. Ethiopians have cooked with teff for thousands of years.

Fast Facts

Africa's exports and imports make up only 4 percent of the world's total exports and imports.

South Africa is the only economically developed country in Africa.

Peanuts are called groundnuts in Africa.

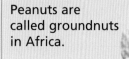

The Past

Indigenous Peoples

*M*any indigenous peoples have lived in Africa for thousands of years. Often, these peoples continue to live as their ancestors did, hunting and gathering, and practicing ancient traditions.

Bedouins are small groups of Arabic **nomads** who tend camels, goats, and sheep in the Sahara Desert. At one time, most of northern Africa's people were Bedouins. Today, less than 10 percent of the area's population are Bedouins. About 20 million Berbers also live in the Sahara. In the past, they lived throughout northern Africa. In the 1600s, Arabs invaded the area, forcing the Berbers to move south. Today, most Berbers live in Morocco's and Algeria's rural areas.

South of the Sahara Desert, most people belong to one of the 800 Black-African cultural groups. Each group has its own language, religion, and way of life. About 70 percent of Black Africans live in rural villages.

Fast Facts

Black Africans account for about 75 percent of Africa's population.

Indigenous groups near the Sahara and in the savannahs of eastern Africa include the Dinka, the Fulani, the Maasai, the Toubou, the Tuareg, and the Turkana. These groups depend on their cattle, sheep, goats, and camels for food.

The Maasai live on the Serengeti Plain, along the Great Rift Valley in Kenya and Tanzania. They are the indigenous peoples of eastern Africa.

The Age of Exploration

Africa was home to many civilizations before Europeans began exploring and claiming parts of the continent. Ancient Egypt began more than 5,000 years ago along the Nile River.

During the 1400s, the Portuguese began exploring Africa's western coast. They wanted to take part in Africa's gold trade. The Portuguese built trading posts in Gambia, Ghana, and other west coast lands. These areas became known as "the Gold Coast."

Beginning in 1569, the Portuguese sent expeditions inland from the coast of Africa to obtain more gold. Gold became one of Africa's most important exports. During the 1600s, the Dutch took control over many Portuguese trading posts on Africa's west coast. In 1652, the Dutch established Cape Town as the first European settlement in South Africa.

By the late 1700s, Europeans began exploring Africa's interior. In 1849, British missionary and explorer David Livingstone crossed the Kalahari Desert from south to north. He traveled across Africa from west to east between 1852 and 1856, exploring the Zambezi River and discovering Victoria Falls.

Fast Facts

In 1497 and 1498, Vasco da Gama sailed to India. He traveled around the Cape of Good Hope, along the eastern coast of Africa.

In 1455, Alvise da Cadamosto reached the mouth of the Gambia River in western Africa. On his second expedition in 1456, he sailed up the Gambia River to the Geba River.

Prince Henry the Navigator was a Portuguese prince who commanded many sailing expeditions along Africa's western coast in the 1400s. However, he did not participate in any voyages.

Early Settlers

The first Europeans to come to Africa were traders and explorers. By the mid-1600s, Dutch settlers arrived near Cape Town's coast in South Africa. This colony was a place where Dutch merchant ships could stop for water and fresh food on their way to the East Indies.

The Dutch farmers became known as Boers. After many years living near the coast, they began moving inland to find more farmland. They used weapons to take control of land where hunter-gatherers called the Khoikboi lived. Boer farmers and ranchers took the Khoikboi's cattle and forced the people to work on Boer farms. The Boers built farms and vineyards on the traditional Khoikboi lands. They continued claiming land until the early 1800s. They did not consider the rights of the indigenous peoples to own the land. The Boers drove away indigenous peoples or forced them to work in poor conditions.

In the mid-1600s, the Dutch East India Company sent explorers to South Africa. The explorers built farms to grow supplies for ships passing along the Cape of Good Hope.

The British took control of Cape Town in the early 1800s. British missionaries wanted to free the Khoikboi from their harsh working conditions. In the 1830s, a small number of Boers rebelled against the British. Many Boers fled the Cape colony. Tens of thousands of Boer farmers traveled by covered wagon over the mountains and into the **veldt**. This became known as the "Great Trek." Bantu peoples lived in the veldt. They did not want the Boers to live on the lands where they herded their cattle. Determined to remain on the land, the Boers fought many times with the Bantu peoples. The Boers built large cattle ranches, farms, and hunting lodges. By the mid-1800s, most of what is now South Africa had been settled.

The Boer Wars (1880 to 1881 and 1899 to 1902) were fought between the British and the Boers.

Culture

Population

Africa's total population is about 875 million people. About 700 million people live south of the Sahara Desert. Just as there are heavily populated areas, there are also areas where few people live. There are large areas of the Sahara and other desert regions where people do not live. Small numbers of people live in some dry grasslands and the tropical rain forests, too.

Crowded African areas include parts of the Mediterranean coast, parts of Nigeria and the west coast, the lake regions of eastern Africa, and the southeast coast. One of the most populated regions on Earth is the Nile River Valley, where about 4,000 people live per square mile (1,550 per sq km).

Africa's population is growing rapidly. Africa has a high birth rate, and since medical care has improved, more babies survive. However, Africa also has a high death rate. Each year, many people die of diseases such as yellow fever, AIDS, sleeping sickness, malaria, and tuberculosis. **Famines**, especially in areas near the Sahara Desert, have killed thousands of people.

In Malawi, severe droughts, flooding, and disease contribute to famine. Only 75 percent of Malawian children live to age 5.

Fast Facts

About two-thirds of Africans live in rural areas. However, since the mid-1900s, millions of people have moved to cities.

Politics and Government

There are many political disputes between Africa's cultural groups and nations. At one time, African countries did not have political boundaries. As boundaries were drawn, land belonging to certain cultural groups was divided. In Africa, people often live in a different country than others in their cultural group. In many cases, several cultural groups now live in the same country. Cultural differences within these countries have caused unrest and even **civil wars** in many African countries.

By the 1880s, there was intense competition between the European powers in Africa. By 1914, most of Africa was divided between Belgium, France, Germany, Great Britain, Italy, Portugal, and Spain. Every part of Africa, except Ethiopia and Liberia, was ruled by European powers. Many Africans did not want to be part of European colonies. By the mid-1900s, many Africans wanted independence. They wanted to elect their own leaders and take control of their own countries.

Between 1950 and 1980, forty-seven African colonies declared independence. However, leaders in many of the new countries faced serious social and economic problems. In some countries, military officers overthrew the governments. Then, military **dictators** took control of the nation, or a single political party became the ruling power.

Today, leaders from all African countries continue to face huge challenges. They must find ways to overcome overpopulation, poverty, disease, and famine.

Fast Facts

Nigeria gained independence from Great Britain on October 1, 1960.

Cleopatra, a well-known Egyptian queen, took the throne in 51 BC. She was only 18 years old.

Nelson Mandela was president of South Africa between 1994 and 1999. He spent 18 years in prison for fighting against apartheid laws.

Cultural Groups

Africa's people come from many cultures, each of which has a long, rich history. In addition to the many indigenous cultural groups, Europeans began settling in parts of Africa in the 1600s. Today, more than five million Africans have European ancestry. Most are British, Dutch, or French.

About one million Asians live in southern and eastern Africa. Their ancestors first came to Africa from India during the 1800s. Madagascar is an island country off Africa's eastern coast. About 2,000 years ago, people from Indonesia began migrating to Madagascar. Today, about 2.5 million people of Asian ancestry live in Madagascar.

Nearly each one of Africa's 800 cultural groups has its own language. Some languages have been spoken for centuries. Traders and settlers brought other languages to Africa from Europe. Certain languages, such as Arabic, Swahili, and Hausa, are spoken by many Africans. Millions of Africans also speak more than one language.

Place Djemma El Fna in Marrakesh, Morocco, is a lively square where vendors sell their wares, food stalls offer local dishes, and performers dance or play music.

There are three language groups in Africa. South of the Sahara Desert, about 290 million people speak the Black-African languages. These include 300 Bantu languages, including Swahili and Zulu. The two main languages of northern Africa are Arabic and Berber. These are Afro-Asian languages. The two main Indo-European languages are Afrikaans and English. Today, three million people speak Afrikaans, a language developed by the Dutch settlers. Nearly three million people speak English, as well.

The official language of many African countries depends on their colonial history. Many countries speak English, French, or Portuguese, for example. Some Africans speak one of the colonial languages, as well as the language of their specific cultural group. This allows them to communicate in business and government situations, as well as within their community.

Fast Facts

Most Europeans living in Africa live along the Mediterranean coast of northern Africa, in the Republic of South Africa, and in Zimbabwe.

The people of Madagascar speak Malagasy.

About 80 million Arabs populate Africa. Some of the areas they live in include Egypt, northern Sudan, and along the Mediterranean coast. Arabs have lived in northern Africa since the 600s.

The Dogon live in the cliffs of southeastern Mali and Burkina Faso. During funeral ceremonies, masked dancers perform on stilts to mimic long-legged water birds.

The Samburu are an indigenous group that lives in northern Kenya. They continue to practice their traditional way of life.

Arts and Entertainment

Music and dance are important to many African cultures. In the Congo (Kinshasa) and Gambia, people enjoy dancing and listening to traditional music featuring drums, xylophones, and string and wind instruments. Kenyans are known for artistic dances they perform during ceremonies to celebrate births, marriages, and funerals. In Kenya, cultural groups compete in traditional dance contests. Popular forms of entertainment in Nigeria are dances that tell stories and dramatic performances. One of the best-known performing groups in South Africa is the vocal group Ladysmith Black Mambazo. They sing a traditional South African music called *Isicathamiya*.

Sculpture is an important African art form. In the ancient Benin Empire, which is now Nigeria, artists created brass sculptures and ivory statues to honor their kings and queens. Kenyans are also well-known for their carved sculptures. The oldest-known African sculptures were found in central Nigeria. These clay figures date back to 500 BC. Wood carvings and bronze and brass figures are also traditional forms of sculpture in Nigeria. The people who live in the forest areas of Cameroon and Nigeria are known for their woodcarvings, such as masks. The Makonde and Zaramo peoples of Tanzania are also known for their carved figures and masks.

Many Egyptian musicians play traditional instruments.

Craftworkers create many different forms of handicrafts. Gold and silver jewelry is made in Guinea, Kenya, and Niger. Woven baskets and rugs are created in Morocco. Leather products are made in Kenya, Ethiopia, Namibia, Zambia, Zimbabwe, Sudan, and Uganda. The Maasai people of Tanzania are known for their leather shields.

North African architecture features Islamic styles. Beautiful domes, mosques, and the designs on jewelry, pottery, rugs, and handicrafts show the influence of their religious beliefs.

Shopkeepers sell pottery in souks, or markets. Marrakesh has the largest Berber market in Morocco.

Fast Facts

Egypt is the center of the Arab motion picture industry.

Storytelling is an important part of the culture in Guinea. Storytellers called griots recite history.

In Somalia, the people enjoy reciting poetry and chanting. Many of their poems tell of classical politics, work, and recreational dance.

In 1986, Nigerian playwright, poet, and novelist Wole Soyinka became the first African writer to win the Nobel Prize in literature.

Dogon masks have influenced many twentieth-century artists, such as Pablo Picasso and Georges Braque.

Sports

*F*ootball is the most popular sport in countries such as Algeria, Congo (Kinshasa), Egypt, Ethiopia, Kenya, Morocco, Nigeria, Somalia, South Africa, Sudan, and Tanzania. In North America, this sport is called soccer. People enjoy watching their favorite teams compete on the field or on television. Many children and adults also play football on amateur sports teams.

Africans enjoy many other sports, too. Track and field is another favorite in countries such as Kenya, Morocco, South Africa, and Tanzania. Africans often excel in running, particularly in long distance running. Many Tanzanians have become world class long distance runners. Kenyan runners have also won many medals in international competitions.

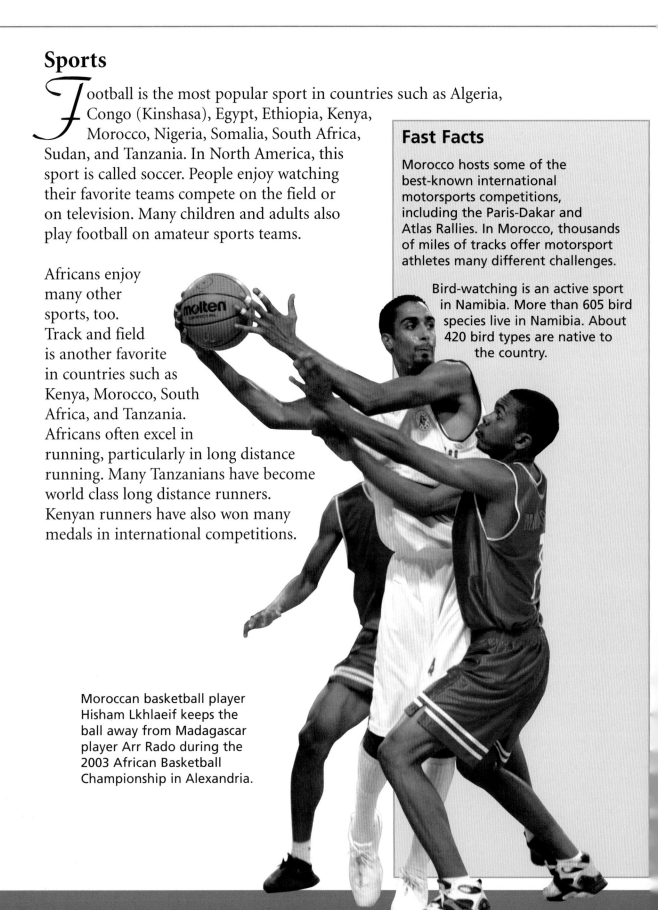

Moroccan basketball player Hisham Lkhlaeif keeps the ball away from Madagascar player Arr Rado during the 2003 African Basketball Championship in Alexandria.

Fast Facts

Morocco hosts some of the best-known international motorsports competitions, including the Paris-Dakar and Atlas Rallies. In Morocco, thousands of miles of tracks offer motorsport athletes many different challenges.

Bird-watching is an active sport in Namibia. More than 605 bird species live in Namibia. About 420 bird types are native to the country.

Basketball is a popular **spectator** sport in Morocco and Niger. Ethiopians enjoy track and field, volleyball, and soccer. Ethiopians also enjoy a game called genna, which is similar to field hockey. Players use bent wooden sticks to move a wooden ball toward a goal. Tennis, lawn bowling, field hockey, boxing, and water sports are popular in South Africa. Other sports South Africans enjoy include cricket, rugby, soccer, and tennis.

Mwera Samwel of Tanzania (second from left), Wilfred Bungei of Kenya (center), and Hezekiel Sepeng of South Africa (second from right) compete in the men's 800-meter race during the 2004 Summer Olympic Games in Athens, Greece.

Brain Teasers

1 How many independent countries and political units are in Africa?

2 Who received the 1993 Nobel Peace Prize for his work to end racism and apartheid in South Africa?

3 Why are the seasons in some African countries opposite to the seasons in other African countries?

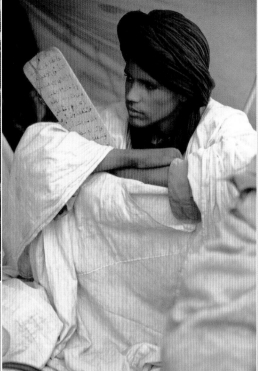

4 What was the name used for Dutch farmers who settled the land of the Khoikboi and then the land of the Bantu peoples in southern Africa?

5 How many languages are spoken in Africa?

6 What is the name of a World Heritage Site in South Africa?

7 What is the name of the world's largest desert?

8 Which African trees have lived for more than 2,000 years?

9 Which nomadic people move their herds of camels, goats, and sheep in search of food and water in the Sahara Desert?

10 What is the name of the first African civilization?

For More Information

Books

Check the school or public library for more information about Africa. The following books have useful information about the continent:

Ayo, Yvonne, Geoff Dann, and Ray Moller. *Eyewitness: Africa.* New York: Dorling Kindersley Publishing, 2000.

Habeeb, William Mark. *Africa Facts & Figures.* Broomall, PA: Mason Crest Publishers, 2004.

Hamilton, Janice. *South Africa in Pictures.* Minneapolis, MN: Lerner Publishing Group, 2003.

Web sites

You can also go online and have a look at the following Web sites:

African Wildlife Foundation
www.awf.org/wildlives

allAfrica.com
http://allafrica.com/

Pyramids: The Inside Story
www.pbs.org/wgbh/nova/pyramid

Lonely Planet Destinations
www.lonelyplanet.com/destinations/loc-afr.htm

Wonders of the African World
www.pbs.org/wonders/index.html

Glossary

ambassador a representative from a country, government, or organization

apartheid an official policy involving unfair treatment for different cultural groups

artifacts objects made in the past by humans

broadleaf having broad, or wide, leaves, rather than needles or scale-like leaves

cassava a starchy root plant

civil wars wars between different regions of the same country

couscous steamed wheat served with a spicy stew of vegetables and meat

dictators rulers who have total control

drought a long period of very low rainfall

equator an imaginary circle around Earth's surface that separates the Northern and Southern Hemispheres

export send goods to other countries to sell or trade

falafel deep-fried spicy patties made of chickpeas

famines drastic, wide-reaching food shortages

hemisphere either the northern half or the southern half of Earth

humid having a high amount of water or water vapor

hummus a dip made of chickpeas, garlic, and lemon

invertebrates animals without backbones

nomads people who move from one place to another in search of food

oasis a fertile or green spot in the desert

okoumé softwood tree used to make furniture and plywood

plantains a large kind of banana

plateau a broad, flat area of high land

political units groups of people with political responsibilities

safaris hunting expeditions or expeditions to take pictures of African animals in their natural habitats

spectator a person who watches an event

veldt rolling, grassy plains of the South African interior

Index

agriculture 11, 15
animals 4, 5, 10, 12, 14, 28, 29
apartheid 5, 21, 28
Arabs 16, 22, 23, 25
art 12, 24, 25, 28

Bantu 19, 23, 29
Bedouins 16, 29
Berbers 16, 22, 23, 25
Black Africans 16, 23
Boers 18, 19, 29

Cadamosto, Alvise da 17
Cape of Good Hope 17, 18, 19
Cape Town, South Africa 13, 17, 18, 19
climate 8, 9
cocoa 10, 11, 14, 15
coffee 14, 15
colonies 18, 19, 21, 23
cotton 11, 14
Cradle of Humankind 12, 13

dancing 23, 24, 25
deserts 5, 6, 8, 9, 10, 11, 12, 13, 16, 17, 20, 23, 29
Dirie, Waris 5
Dogon 23, 25

economy 12, 15, 21
Egypt 4, 6, 13, 17, 23, 24, 25, 26, 29
equator 6, 9, 29
Ethiopia 4, 5, 11, 14, 21, 25, 26, 27
explorers 17, 18, 19

famine 20, 21
farm 11, 14, 15, 18, 19, 29
food 5, 15, 16, 18, 29
foreign aid 15
forests 4, 8, 9, 10, 11, 12, 14, 20, 24

Gama, Vasco da 17
grasslands 4, 8, 9, 10, 14, 20
Great Rift Valley 5, 9, 16
Great Sphinx 13
Great Trek 19

Kalahari Desert 8, 17
Keino, Kipchoge 5
Khoikboi 18, 19, 29

Ladysmith Black Mambazo 24
languages 16, 22, 23, 28, 29
Livingstone, David 17

Maasai 16, 25
Madagascar 9, 19, 22, 23, 26, 27
Mandela, Nelson 5, 21, 29
manufacturing 14, 15
minerals 11, 14, 15
mining 14
Morocco 16, 22, 25, 26, 27
mountains 8, 9, 10, 19
music 24

Nile River 9, 13, 17, 20

oceans 6, 8, 13, 19

plants 4, 10, 13, 14
plateau 8

politics 4, 21, 25
population 4, 16, 20, 21, 23
Prince Henry the Navigator 17
pyramids 13

rain forests 4, 8, 9, 10, 12, 20

safari 12
Sahara Desert 5, 8, 9, 11, 16, 20, 23, 29
Samburu 8, 23
savannah 9, 10, 12, 16
sports 5, 26, 27
storytelling 25

tourism 12
trade 10, 15, 17, 18, 22
transportation 15